MAKE ME LAUGH!

SCHOOLYARD SNICKERS

Classy Jokes That Make the Grade

by Sam Schultz
pictures by Brian Gable

Carolrhoda Books, Inc. • Minneapolis

Mother: Why did you get such a low grade on your test today, Barry?

Barry: The kid who sits next to me was absent.

First Student: How did you do with the test questions?

Second Student: I did fine with the questions. It's the answers I had trouble with!

2

Teacher: Why are you running?

Boy: I'm running to stop a fight.

Teacher: Between who?

Boy: Between me and the guy who's chasing me!

Teacher: In what battle did General Wolfe cry, "I die happy"?

Student: His last one.

Arnie: I wish I had been born a thousand years ago.

Les: Why?

Arnie: Just think of all the history I wouldn't have to study!

Billy: Why weren't you in school today?

Willy: I had a toothache so I went to the dentist.

Billy: Does your tooth still ache?

Willy: I don't know. The dentist kept it!

Q: What's worse than finding a worm in your apple?

A: Finding half a worm!

Daughter: Dad, can you write your name in the dark?

Dad: I think so.

Daughter: Great. Would you please turn off the lights and sign my report card?

Teacher: All these homework problems in math are wrong.

Student: Better not let my dad find out.

Teacher: Why not? Will he punish you?

Student: No. He told me math was his best subject!

Billy's Mother: Billy told me he got 100 on his tests yesterday!

Billy's Teacher: He did. 50 in spelling and 50 in arithmetic.

Teacher: What do you call a horse doctor?

Student: A doctor with a sore throat.

Teacher: Where do we get milk?

Student: From the supermarket!

Jack: What's the toughest thing for you in school?

Mack: Trying to whisper to the kid next to me without moving my lips.

Science Teacher: Who can tell me what an atom is?

Student: Isn't that the guy who went with Eve?

Sister: How have you been doing in school, Bobby?

Bobby: Well, I've been working hard to get ahead.

Sister: That's good. You could certainly use one.

Teacher: Joan, if I had six oranges in one hand and seven in the other, what would I have?

Joan: Very big hands!

Teacher: This is the fifth time this week I've had to punish you. What do you have to say for yourself?

Student: Thank goodness it's Friday.

Teacher: What's the capital of Alaska?

Emma: Juneau?

Teacher: Of course I do, but I'm asking you!

Student: I don't think I deserve a zero on this test.

Teacher: Neither do I. But it's the lowest grade I can give you.

Mother: Lois, why are you crying?

Lois: My teacher yelled at me for something I didn't do.

Mother: What was it you didn't do?

Lois: My homework!

Teacher: Will you two stop passing notes!

Student: We're not passing notes. We're playing cards!

Q: What's bacteria?

A: The rear entrance to the cafeteria.

Father: Arnie, your teacher told me you're at the bottom of the class.

Arnie: So what, Dad? We learn the same things at both ends.

Teacher: Why are the Middle Ages called the Dark Ages?

Student: Because there were so many knights.

Teacher: Children, open your geography books. Who can tell me where South America is?

Student: I know! It's on page 15.

Teacher: What's the definition of dogma?

Student: A dogma is a puppy's mother.

Tom: I won't be coming to school tomorrow. I'll be home sick.

John: I didn't know you were sick.

Tom: I will be after my mom sees my report card!

Teacher: Donald, I hope I didn't see you looking at Andy's paper.

Donald: I hope you didn't either!

Grandma: Tell me what you did in school today.

Ted: We did Adzuptus.

Grandma: Really? How do you do that?

Ted: One and one adzupto two, two and two adzupto four.

Mother: I know my daughter talks a lot in class, but she is trying.

Teacher: She certainly is!

Teacher: How do you know the earth is round?

Student: Why are you asking me? I never said it was.

Mother: How do you like school, Cathy?

Cathy: Closed.

Teacher: Well, there's one good thing I can say about your son.

Father: Oh? What's that?

Teacher: With grades like his, he can't possibly be cheating!

Boy on Phone: Mom, they're starving us here at boarding school.

Mom: Oh dear! What are they feeding you?

Boy: Just breakfast, lunch, and dinner!

Q: Who knows what an echo is?

A: Could you repeat the question?

Teacher: Ernie, I thought I told you I never want to see you walk into this classroom late again.

Ernie: I know, that's why I'm crawling in!

Teacher: If you have three chocolate bars and I ask you to give me one, how many will you have left?

Student: Three.

Q: What's a barbarian?

A: That's the guy who cuts your hair in the library!

There once was a teacher named Bass,
Who stood at the head of the class.
And he said with a smirk,
"Those who don't do homework
Get a party on me if they pass!"

Mike: My boy scout troop had to carry an old lady across the street yesterday.

Teacher: Why did you have to carry her?

Mike: Because she didn't want to go!

Q: Where do dates grow?

A: On calendar trees.

Teacher: I'd like to go just one day without having to make you stay after school!

Student: OK, permission granted.

Mothers: Johnny, I hope you're not talking in class anymore since your teacher sent me that note.

Johnny: Nope. Not any more, but not any less, either!

Teacher: A,B,C,D,E,F,G. What comes after G?

Student: Whiz.

Chris: Mom, could you help me with my math homework?

Mom: No, Chris, it wouldn't be right.

Chris: That's okay, as long as you give it a try!

Teacher: Jerry, don't you have something to tell me?

Jerry: No, ma'am.

Teacher: Didn't you miss school yesterday?

Jerry: Not a bit. I had a lot of fun!

Teacher: Jackie, you've been late to school every day since school began. What's the reason?

Jackie: I can't help it. The sign on the street says, "School, go slow."

Q: Where was the Declaration of Independence signed?

A: At the bottom.

Teacher: When you think of Greece, what's the first thing that comes to your mind?

Student: French fries.

Teacher: Sandy, you spelled that word perfectly. Did you read the dictionary?

Sandy: No, but I saw the movie.

Teacher: Danny, let's pretend you're a big game hunter, and you suddenly come across an alligator, a lion, and a rhinoceros. Which one would you get fur from?

Danny: I'd get as fur from all of them as I could get!

Q: Who knows the president of France?

A: The president's wife.

A teacher asked her class to make a list of the nine greatest living Americans.

Teacher: Are you finished with your list yet, Pete?

Pete: Not yet. I still have to think of a third baseman.

Q: Did you hear about the little boy who runs home every day after school?

A: He's trying to make the Guiness Book of World Records for the kid with the most home runs!

It was the first day of school after Christmas vacation.

Mother: Mary, explain why you got a 60 on this math test!

Mary: Oh, our teacher always marks things down after Christmas.

Jerry: I'm not going to school today, Mom. Nobody there likes me.

Mother: That's nonsense, Jerry. Besides, you have to go to school today. You're the principal!

Teacher: Joseph, you didn't wash your face this morning, did you? I can see you had eggs for breakfast.

Joseph: No I didn't, ma'am. I had cereal. I had eggs yesterday!

Q: Who won at Bull Run?

A: I don't know. Was the score in the papers?

Teacher: Susie, you don't seem to be paying any attention to me. Are you having trouble hearing?

Susie: No, I'm having trouble listening!

School would really be okay
If we had an extra holiday.
Or two, or three, or maybe ten.
School might not be so awful then.
Another thing that would be cool
Is having Friday off from school!

Larry: My mother's going to night school.

Teacher: Really? Why?

Larry: I don't know. I guess she wants to learn to read in the dark!

A third-grade class went to a museum. On a glass case with a mummy in it, there was a sign that said, "400 B.C."

Teacher: Who can tell the class what the sign means?

Student: That's the license number of the car that hit him!

Q: Who knows something about Buddha?

A: That's what we used before my mother switched to margarine.

Voice on Phone: Is this the principal?

Principal: Yes.

Voice on Phone: Jenny Smith is too sick to come to school today.

Principal: Who's calling, please?

Voice on Phone: This is my mother.

Alice: Mom, my teacher told me not to take any more baths!

Mother: Are you sure that's what she said?

Alice: Well, she told me to stay out of hot water or she'd keep me after school!

Teacher: Teddy, you come right up here and give me what you've got in your mouth.

Teddy: I don't think you'd want it, teacher. It's a toothache!

The teacher had just handed out report cards.

Billy: Miss Jones, I don't want to scare you, but my dad told me that if I don't take home a good report card, somebody's going to get spanked!

Teacher: Dennis, what should I do about you? You never get to school on time.

Dennis: Just don't wait, ma'am. Go ahead and start without me.

Teacher: Mary, tell your classmates what you share with your parents.

Mary: My homework.

Father: How was school today?

Son: It wouldn't be so bad if my teacher wasn't so dumb.

Father: What do you mean?

Son: All she does all day long is ask us silly questions.

Teacher: Johnny, if you take 2 from 5, and 2 from 6, what's the difference?

Johnny: I know what you mean. It doesn't make any difference to me, either.

Jimmy: My brother goes to college.

Teacher: Really? What does he take?

Jimmy: Anything Mom and Pop will give him.

Q: How would you find the English Channel?

A: By turning the dial on the television set.

Teacher: I wish you'd pay a little attention to me, Sally.

Sally: I am. As little as possible!

Father: What does this "F" on your report card mean?

Student: "Fantastic!"

Father: How do you like your new school, Rodney?

Rodney: I don't think I'm going to like it, Dad. It's haunted.

Father: That's silly. Who told you that?

Rodney: The teacher. He keeps talking about the school spirit.

Mother: What did you learn in school today?

Child: My teacher taught us writing.

Mother: What did you write?

Child: I don't know. She hasn't taught us reading yet.

Teacher: Ronnie, why is it so difficult for you to learn how to spell?

Ronnie: Because you keep changing the words!

Teacher: Timmy, if you were standing in California, which would be the farthest away, New York City or the moon?

Timmy: New York City.

Teacher: What makes you say that?

Timmy: I can see the moon, but I can't see New York City!

Q: How do you spell Mississippi?

A: The river or the state?

Betsy: Mom, you won't have to buy me any new schoolbooks next year.

Mom: That's good news. Why not?

Betsy: Because my teacher didn't pass me.

Teacher: Did your father help you with these arithmetic problems?

Student: No, sir. I got them wrong all by myself.

Father: (Sternly) I received a note from your teacher today, Jeffrey.

Jeffrey: That's okay, Pop. I won't tell Mom.

Teacher: Brian told me you threw a rock through my classroom window.

Tim: It's not my fault, it's Brian's fault.

Teacher: Why is it Brian's fault?

Tim: When I threw the rock at him, he ducked!

Teacher: Tommy, if you could save a dollar a week for a whole year, what would you have?

Tommy: I'd have a new bike!

Teacher: William, did Ellen help you with these arithmetic problems?

William: No, ma'am.

Teacher: Are you sure?

William: Honest, she didn't help me. She did them all herself.

Q: Do you know Lincoln's Gettysburg Address?

A: I thought he lived in the White House.

Teacher: Marty, why haven't you returned your report card?

Marty: Because you gave me two A's. My parents are still showing it to all the relatives!

Q: What did George Washington, Abraham Lincoln, and Christopher Columbus have in common?

A: They were all born on holidays.

Johnny: Teacher, I ain't got a pencil.

Teacher: Johnny, I haven't got a pencil.

Johnny: That makes two of us.

Bus Driver: Do you want to go to Fifth Street School?

Little Girl: No. I have to.

Q: What's the difference between a schoolteacher and a train engineer?

A: A schoolteacher trains the mind, and a train engineer minds the train.

Teacher: How many months have 28 days?

Student: All of them.

Johnny: Mom, my teacher said my penmanship is awful.

Mom: Then why don't you practice and make it better?

Johnny: No. Then she'll figure out I can't spell!

This book is available in two editions:
Library binding by Carolrhoda Books, Inc., a division of Lerner Publishing Group
Soft cover by First Avenue Editions, an imprint of Lerner Publishing Group
241 First Avenue North
Minneapolis, MN 55401 U.S.A.

Website address: www.lernerbooks.com

Library of Congress Cataloging-in-Publication Data

Schultz, Sam.
    Schoolyard snickers : classy jokes that make the grade / by Sam Schultz ;
illustrations by Brian Gable.
      p.   cm. — (Make me laugh)
    ISBN: 1–57505–643–7 (lib. bdg. : alk. paper)
    ISBN: 1–57505–707–7 (pbk. : alk. paper)
    1. Education—Juvenile humor. 2. Schools—Juvenile humor. [1. Schools—
Humor. 2. Jokes. 3. Riddles. 4. Puns and punning.] I. Gable, Brian, 1949– ill.
II. Title. III. Series.
PN6231.S3 S85 2004
818'.5402—dc21   2002151106

Manufactured in the United States of America
1 2 3 4 5 6 – JR – 09 08 07 06 05 04